Living and Nonliving in
Polar Regions

Rebecca Rissman

Raintree is an imprint of Capstone Global Library Limited, a company incorporated in England and Wales having its registered office at 7 Pilgrim Street, London, EC4V 6LB – Registered company number: 6695582

www.raintreepublishers.co.uk
myorders@raintreepublishers.co.uk

Edited by Daniel Nunn, Rebecca Rissman, and Catherine Veitch
Designed by Cynthia Della-Rovere
Picture research by Tracy Cummins
Production by Sophia Argyris
Originated by Capstone Global Library Ltd
Printed and bound in China by Leo Paper Products Ltd

ISBN 978 1 406 26591 0 (hardback)
17 16 15 14 13
10 9 8 7 6 5 4 3 2 1

ISBN 978 1 406 26598 9 (paperback)
18 17 16 15 14
10 9 8 7 6 5 4 3 2 1

British Library Cataloguing in Publication Data
A full catalogue record for this book is available from the British Library.

Acknowledgements
We would like to thank the following for permission to reproduce photographs: Getty Images pp. 10 (© Eastcott Momatiuk), 16, 23c (© Paul Nicklen); istockphoto p. 22 (© Dmitry Deshevykh); Shutterstock pp. 1, 6, 23b (© Christopher Wood), 4, 23e, 23f (© Bruce Rolff), 5 (© hallam creations), 7 (© BMJ), 8 (© Bronwyn Photo), 9, 11 (© Volodymyr Goinyk), 12, 23a (© Maksym Deliyergiyev), 13 (© dalish), 14, 23d (© yui), 15 (© Eirik Johan Solheim), 18 (© Virginija Valatkiene), 19 (© zahradales), 20 (© Gentoo Multimedia Ltd.), 21 (© Patrick Poendl), 23g (© Galyna Andrushko); Superstock p. 17 (© Minden Pictures).

Front cover photograph of Adelie penguin on iceberg in Antarctica reproduced with permission of Superstock (© Minden Pictures).

We would like to thank Michael Bright and Diana Bentley for their invaluable help in the preparation of this book.

Every effort has been made to contact copyright holders of material reproduced in this book. Any omissions will be rectified in subsequent printings if notice is given to the publisher.

All the Internet addresses (URLs) given in this book were valid at the time of going to press. However, due to the dynamic nature of the Internet, some addresses may have changed, or sites may have changed or ceased to exist since publication. While the author and publisher regret any inconvenience this may cause readers, no ~~responsibility for any such changes can be accepted by~~ ~~either the author or the publisher.~~

Some words are in bold, **like this**.
You can find them in the glossary on page 23.

Contents

What are the polar regions?

The polar regions are areas on Earth that are very cold.

The polar regions are close to the **north** and **south poles**.

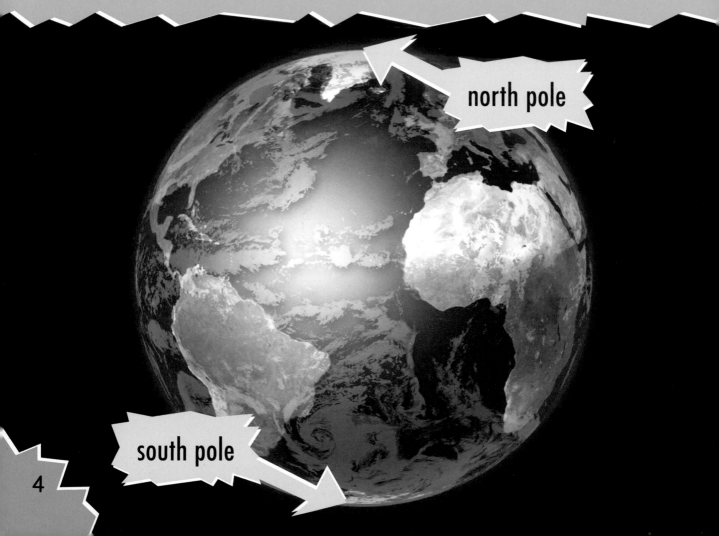

north pole

south pole

Different types of plants and animals live in the polar regions.

There are **non-living** things in the polar regions, too.

What are living things?

Living things are alive. Living things need air and **sunlight**. Living things need food and water.

Living things move on their own.

Living things grow and change.

What are non-living things?

Non-living things are not alive. Non-living things do not need air and **sunlight**.

Non-living things do not need food and water.

Non-living things do not grow and change on their own.

Non-living things do not move on their own.

Is a seal living or non-living?

A seal needs food and water.

A seal moves on its own.

A seal grows and changes.

A seal needs air and **sunlight**.

A seal is **living**.

Is lichen living or non-living?

Lichen needs water.

Lichen moves on its own towards the sun.

Lichen grows and changes.

Lichen needs air and **sunlight**.

Lichen is **living**.

Is a rock living or non-living?

A rock does not grow on its own.

A rock does not need air or **sunlight**.

A rock does not need food or water.

A rock does not move on its own.

A rock is **non-living**.

Is a narwhal living or non-living?

A **narwhal** grows and changes.

A narwhal needs food and water.

A narwhal needs air and **sunlight**.

A narwhal moves on its own.

A narwhal is **living**.

Is ice living or non-living?

Ice does not move on its own.

Ice does not need food.

Ice does not grow.

Ice does not need air or **sunlight**.

Ice is **non-living**.

Is a penguin living or non-living?

A penguin grows and changes.

A penguin needs air and **sunlight**.

A penguin needs food and water.

A penguin moves on its own.

A penguin is **living**.

What do you think?

Is this fox **living** or **non-living**?

Glossary

lichen
simple plant

north pole
the place
furthest north
on Earth

living alive. Living
things need food and
water. They breathe,
move on their own,
grow, and change.

south pole
the place
furthest south
on Earth

narwhal
type of whale

sunlight
light from
the sun

non-living not alive.
Non-living things do not need
food or water. They do not
move on their own, or grow
and change.

Find out more

Websites

Click through these images of living and non-living things, then take a quiz!
www.bbc.co.uk/schools/scienceclips/ages/5_6/ourselves.shtml

Check out this site to learn more about what living things need.
www.kidsbiology.com/biology_basics/needs_living_things/living_things_have_needs1.php

Go to this site and try to spot all the living things in the park!
www.sciencekids.co.nz/gamesactivities/plantsanimals.html

Books

The Arctic Habitat (Introducing Habitats), Molly Aloian and Bobbie Kalman (Crabtree, 2006)

Living and Nonliving, Carol K. Lindeen (Capstone Press, 2008)

Polar Regions (Habitats of the World), Alison Ballance (Dominie Press, 2004)

Index